First Reconciliation

Activities for Primary Grades

Pflaum Publishing Group
Dayton, OH 45439

First Reconciliation

Activities for Primary Grades

Activities are by Francine M. O'Connor, the author of numerous books, articles, and programs for children. Francine was managing editor of Liguorian Magazine for eighteen years before her retirement to upstate New York to be with her family. Currently, she serves as DRE for St. Francis of Assisi Parish in Potsdam and prepares second graders for their first receptions of Eucharist and Reconciliation.

Activities on pages 8, 9, 12, 15, 17, and 18 by Jean Larkin

Cover Design by Elaine Tannenbaum
Interior Design and Illustrations by Patricia Lynch and Linda Becker
Edited by Jean Larkin

ISBN: 1-933178-09-4
Stock Code: 3451

Contents

How to Use This Book 4

We Are Family

What Makes You Happy? 5
Following God 6
Building Blocks of Love 7
Rules Rebus 8-9
Jesus' Love in Motion 10
The Most Happy People 11

Sometimes We Fail

Accident, Mistake, or Sin? 12
The Key to Forgiveness 13
Turning Bad into Good 14
Forgive—Times Seven 15
Signs of Peace 16
Listen to Your Heart 17
Fresh Starts 18

We Confess and Are Forgiven

My Reconciliation Book 19-20
Meeting the Forgiving Jesus 21-22
I'm Sorry 23
I Follow Good Advice 24
A Special Gift 25

We Try Harder

Hidden Messages 26
Stop, Look, Listen, Act 27
A Maze of Decisions 28
Staying Strong 29
Staying Close to Jesus 30

Answers and Notes 31-32

How to Use This Book

These activities were developed to complement any formal program you may be using to prepare primary grade children for their first reception of the Sacrament of Reconciliation. The goal was to make all the activities suitable for this age group. As you know, however, not all children are the same. You may think some of the activities are too challenging for some of the children and not challenging enough for others.

Use your own judgment regarding which activities to use and, in some cases, which parts of the activity to use. For instance, the activity "Hidden Messages" on page 26 requires the children to find words within the word *temptation*. Answers can be two-letter, three-letter, or four-letter words. You may tell the children to find just the two-letter words or all of the words.

Progression

The activities move from page to page in a progression: foundational rules that lead us to God; acknowledgement of our need to forgive and be forgiven; confession that leads to reconciliation; and avoiding temptation. You may choose, however, to use the activities in whatever order best serves your needs. For instance, on page 10, there is a pantomime prayer activity that helps the children remember the two Great Commandments. You may want to use this first so the children can learn it and use it to begin each session.

Scripture

If an activity is based on a part or parts of Scripture, the citation is given for your reference, either in the activity itself or on pages 31-32. In some cases, the text is a paraphrase of the passage to enable the children to better understand its meaning.

Extending Activities

The last two pages of this book not only supply the answers to the puzzles and list supplies needed but they suggest ways to extend some of the activities with the children. Ideas for initiating further discussion, for developing a subject more broadly, and for clarifying certain parts of the teaching are also given.

Enjoy!

This book is meant to provide activities that will engage children in a positive way while reinforcing what they are learning about the sacrament. The goal is to make the activities fun, enjoyable, and, at the same time, reverent and rewarding. We hope you enjoy using them in this same spirit.

Name ______________________________

What Makes You Happy?

Finish each of these sentences by putting a circle around either the happy or the sad face. For #10, write your own example of what makes you happy.

1. When I do my best in school, I feel . . .  

2. When Mom says, "I forgive you" and hugs me, I feel . . .  

3. When our family plays games together, I feel . . .  

4. When I argue with my friends, I feel . . .  

5. When I get a kiss good night, I feel . . . 

6. When I disobey my parents, I feel . . .  

7. When Dad has to remind me to clean my room, I feel . . .  

8. When I remember how much God loves me, I feel . . .  

9. When I tell a lie, I feel . . .  

10. ______________________________

____

Name____

Following God

When you were baptized into God's family, your parents and godparents promised to teach you about God.

Solve the acrostic puzzle below to find out what Jesus said about people who follow God's laws. First, write the answers to the picture clues on the numbered blanks. Then, transfer those letters to the same-numbered blanks in the quote below.

"Whoever does the will of my Father in heaven is. . .

___ ___   ___ ___ ___ ___ ___ ___ ___   ___ ___ ___
1 2   3 4 5 6 7 8 9   10 11 12

___ ___ ___ ___ ___ ___   ___ ___ ___   ___ ___ ___ ___ ___ ___."
13 14 15 16 17 18   19 20 21   22 23 24 25 26 27

Matthew 12:50

Name ____________________

Building Blocks of Love

Every day, the people who love you help you to follow God's ways. Look at these pictures and the captions below. Each caption is a message that Jesus gave us. Cut out each caption and paste it below the correct picture. You'll see how you are learning to live like Jesus.

"Love one another as I have loved you."	"Teach them all that I have taught you."	"Pray always."
"When two or three gather in prayer, I am with you."	"Forgive others."	"Give to those who are poor."

Name ____

Rules Rebus (Part 1)

Families have rules. Schools have rules. Games have rules. Rules keep things fair. Rules help things run more smoothly. God also has rules. If everyone follows God's rules, we will all live together in peace and love. First, we need to know, love, and respect God. So God gave us these rules.

Love God

I am your God. You should love me above all other people and things.

My name is sacred. Always use it with care.

Sunday is a special day of the week to be with me.

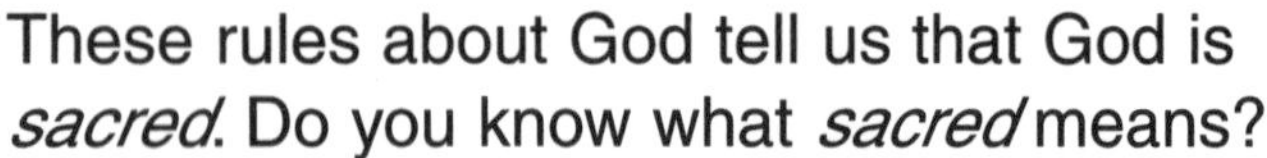

These rules about God tell us that God is *sacred*. Do you know what *sacred* means? To find out, solve this rebus, using the line below to work on.

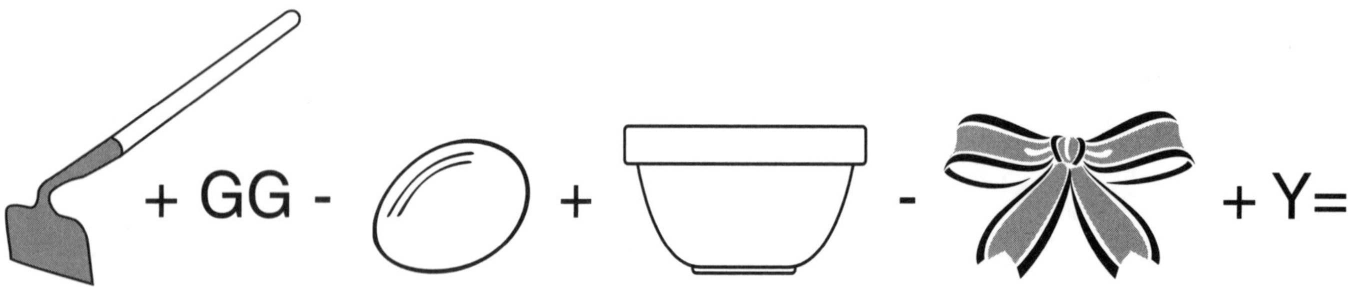

____

Go on to Part 2 of this activity to learn God's rules for getting along with one another.

Name ______________________________

Rules Rebus (Part 2)

The first rules God gave us taught us to know, love, and stay close to God. But there are more rules to learn if we want to live in peace. We need to know, love, and get along with others. So God gave us these rules.

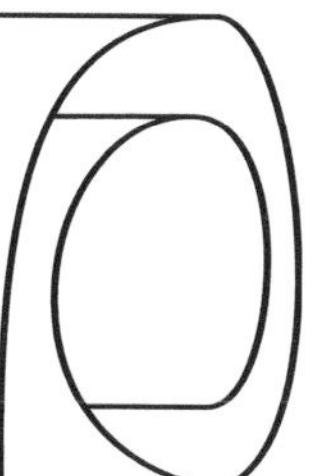

Love One Another

Honor your father and mother.

Be kind to other people. Never hurt them in any way.

Be faithful and loyal to those you love.

Honor what belongs to others. Take only what belongs to you.

Always tell the truth.

Be happy for the blessings of others.

These rules talk about honoring other people and what belongs to them. Do you know what *honor* means? To find out, solve this rebus, using the line below to work on.

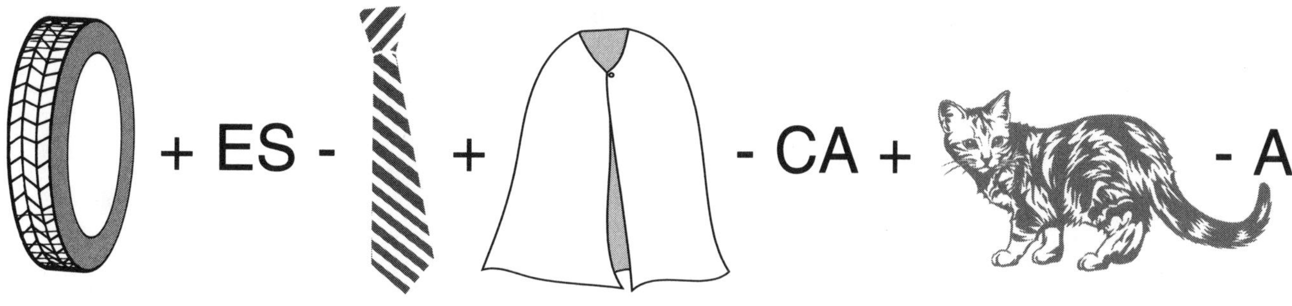

____

Name ____________________

Jesus' Love In Motion

Here is a special way to remember Jesus' two Great Commandments.
As you read the words of the poem below, learn and follow the actions together.

I'll love God with
all my heart,

in the way God loved
me from the start.

I'll love God with
all my soul

with a love that comes
complete and whole.

I'll love God with
my mind today,

in all that I think
and all that I say.

I'll love all my
neighbors too,

like you and you
and you and you.

I'll love myself, a
creature of God,

who made us all
to live in love.

Name ____

The Most Happy People

It seems that some people are always happy, even if things go wrong. How can that be? Jesus told us the ways to be happy. These ways are called the Beatitudes.

Follow these steps to make a Happiness Plate, which will help you remember these special ways to happiness.

1) Color the border of your plate with bright, happy colors.
2) Sign your name on the line, showing that you want to be a happy person too.
3) Cut out the plate and glue it to a bright circle of construction paper.
4) Punch a hole in the top of your plate, and string yarn or ribbon through the hole.
5) Hang your Happiness Plate where it will always remind you how to be happy.

Name ______________________________

Accident, Mistake, or Sin?

When something happens and we didn't mean it to, that is called an accident.

When we make a wrong choice or give a wrong answer because we didn't know the right choice or answer, that is called a mistake.

When we do something that we know God told us not to do, that is called a sin.

It is important to know the difference between an accident, a mistake, and a sin. Read each of these sentences and decide which answer is correct.

(Check One)

1. Jason was careless and spilled a glass of milk at the breakfast table. Accident____ Mistake____ Sin____

2. Latisha told her mother she had fed the dog, but she had not. Accident____ Mistake____ Sin____

3. Su Linn wrote down the wrong phone number while taking a message. Accident____ Mistake____ Sin____

4. Manuel took money from his dad's wallet without asking him. Accident____ Mistake____ Sin____

5. Samuel kicked his soccer ball too hard and it broke his neighbor's window. Accident____ Mistake____ Sin____

Name ______________________________

The Key to Forgiveness

Jesus came to forgive our sins. If we want to follow Jesus in everything we do, we must do what Jesus told us about forgiveness. Use the Key below and discover what letter each symbol stands for. Write that letter on the correct line. You will then know the promise Jesus made to us about forgiveness.

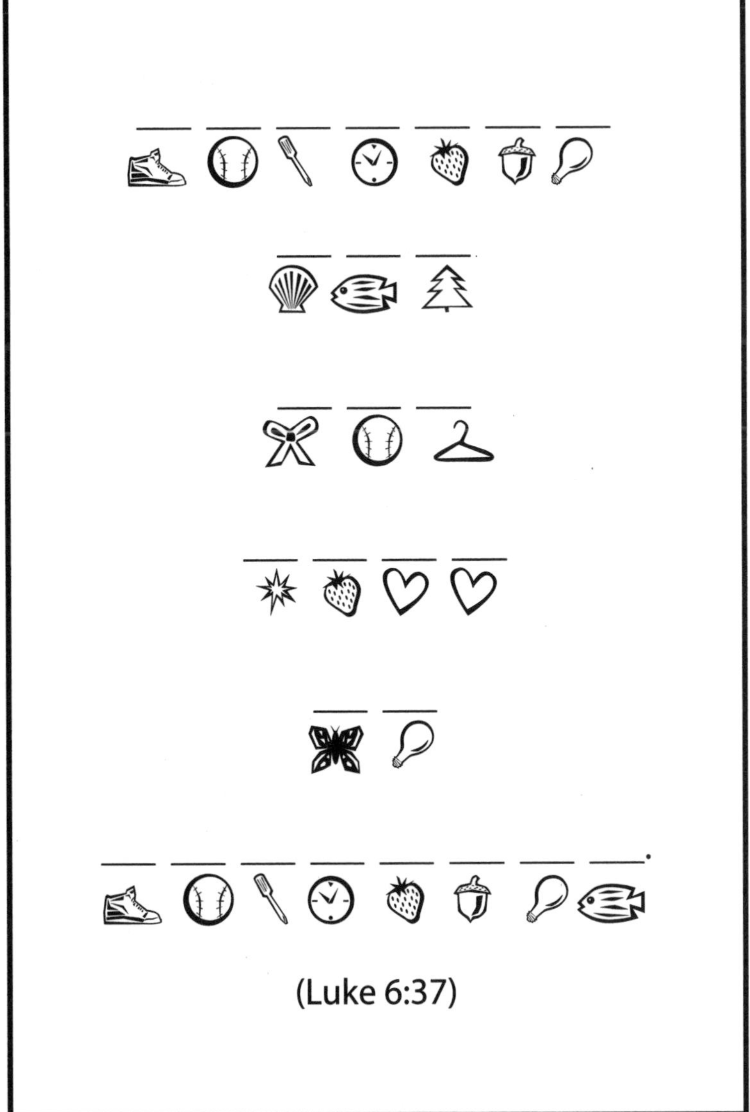

Key

= A
= B
= D
= E
= F
= G
= I
= L
= N
= O
= R
= U
= V
= W
= Y

Name ____________________

Turning Bad into Good

It is not always easy to forgive someone who hurts us in some way. Jesus often talked about how we should behave when someone is mean to us or makes us sad. Jesus told us how to turn those bad things into good things.

Look at each pair of words below. Choose the right pair to complete each of these sentences. Or, using these same pairs, write sentences of your own that turn something bad into something good.

1. __ __ __ __ your __ __ __ __ __ __ __.

2. __ __ __ __ __ __ to those who __ __ __ __ you.

3. __ __ __ __ __ those who __ __ __ __ __ you.

4. __ __ __ __ for those who __ __ __ __ __ __ __ __ you.

Word Pairs

BLESS/CURSE • DO GOOD/HATE • LOVE/ENEMIES • PRAY/MISTREAT

Write some of your own ideas for turning bad into good.

Name ______________________________

Forgive–Times Seven

One day Jesus said to his disciples, "Forgive people who say they are sorry when they do wrong. Even if someone mistreats you seven times in one day and says, 'I am sorry,' you should forgive that person." (See Luke 17:3-4.)

The number seven had a special meaning in those days. It meant a number so big you couldn't count that high. Jesus used the number seven to mean we must forgive one another over and over and over again, just as God forgives us.

See if you can find the word FORGIVE seven times in this puzzle. It could be up, down, diagonal, left to right, or right to left.

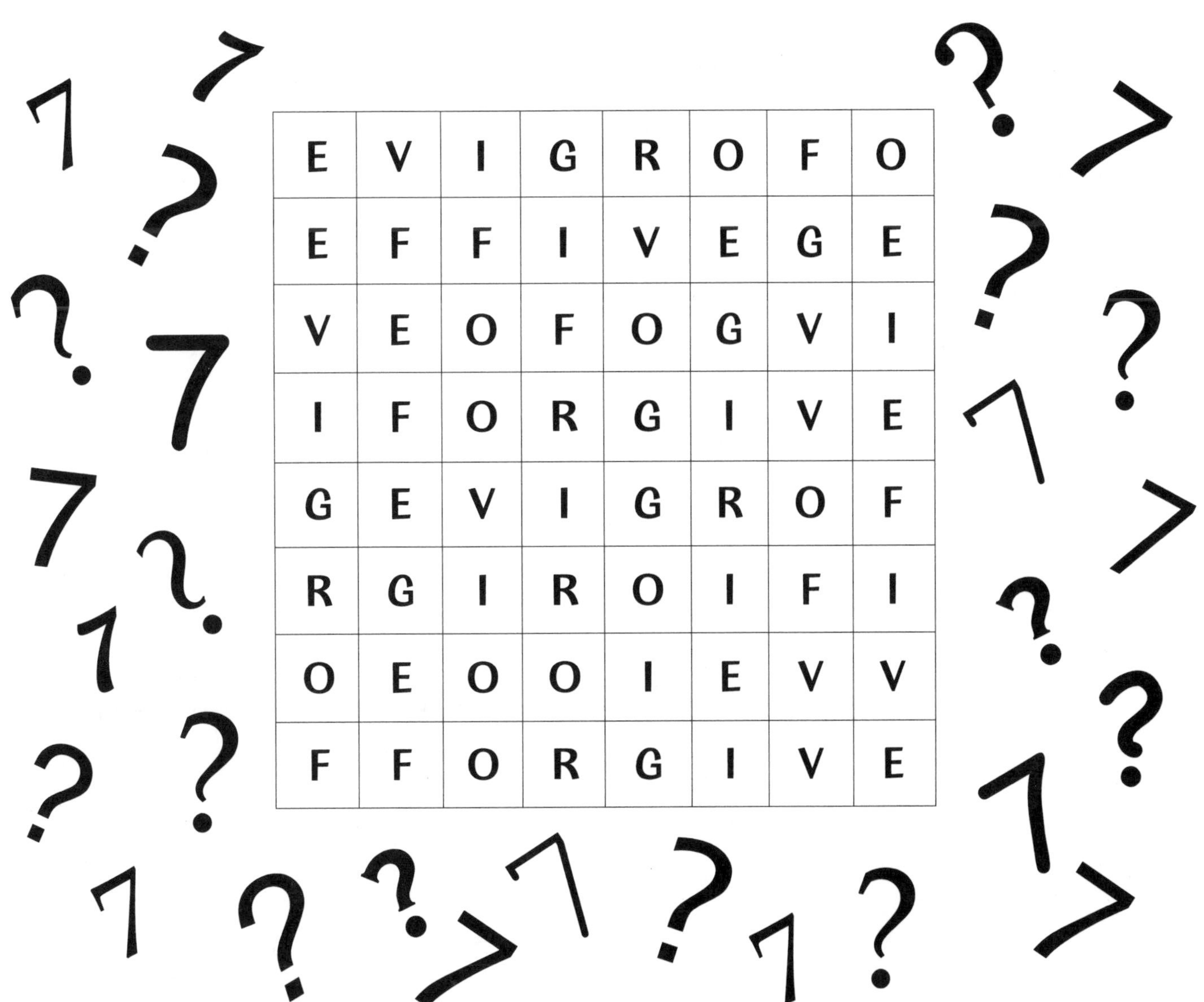

E	V	I	G	R	O	F	O
E	F	F	I	V	E	G	E
V	E	O	F	O	G	V	I
I	F	O	R	G	I	V	E
G	E	V	I	G	R	O	F
R	G	I	R	O	I	F	I
O	E	O	O	I	E	V	V
F	F	O	R	G	I	V	E

Name ____

Signs of Peace

Reconciliation happens whenever people say two magic phrases: “I am sorry” and “I forgive you.” Think about a time when you “made up” with someone and felt at peace again with that person. What did you do to show you were friends again?

People use different signs to show they are reconciled and at peace. Draw a line from the picture in the first column to the people who might use that sign in the second column.

NATIVE AMERICANS

YOUR FRIENDS

YOUR PARENTS

LEADERS OF COUNTRIES

YOU AND GOD

Name ____

Listen to Your Heart

Learning to choose right from wrong is something we all have to learn. God gave us rules to guide us, and parents and teachers to help us learn when to say yes and when to say no.

But we all have something special inside us that also helps us know how to choose between right and wrong. For instance, when you are tempted to tell a lie, if you listen deep within your heart, you will hear, "It is wrong to lie. Always tell the truth." There is a special name for this "little voice" in your heart.

Start at the arrow and write down every other letter until you have used them all. The solved puzzle will tell you what your "little voice" is called.

__ __ __ __ __ __ __ __ __ __ __ __ __

__ __ __ __ __ __ __ __ __ __ __.

Name ______________________________

Fresh Starts

When you are doing homework, do you ever write the wrong answer and have to erase it to start over?

When you are making your bed, does the sheet or blanket ever get crooked and you have to start over?

When you are playing kick ball, does the ball ever go over the fence and then you have to start over?

Many times we need to start over to make something right or better. We call these times "fresh starts."

When we commit a sin, we have to make a fresh start with God. We do this when we receive a special sacrament that has three names! But all three names are mixed up below. They all need a fresh start! See if you can unscramble the letters and discover the three names of this sacrament.

PENANEC

___ ___ ___ ___ ___ ___ ___

CONFSEISNO

___ ___ ___ ___ ___ ___ ___ ___ ___ ___

RECONITCLAIION

___ ___ ___ ___ ___ ___ ___ ___ ___ ___ ___ ___ ___ ___

PRAYER AFTER CONFESSION

Dear Jesus,

Thank you for being with me in a special way as I confessed my sins today.

I am so happy that you have forgiven me for doing wrong, and I promise that I will try to do better in the future.

Thank you for speaking to me through the priest. As I carry out the penance he gave me, remember that I love you and always want to be close to you.

Amen

I made my First Reconciliation at

________________________parish.

Date:________________________

PRAYER BEFORE CONFESSION

Dear Jesus,

Thank you for your love and forgiveness.

I want to make a good confession today. Please help me to remember my sins, be sorry for them, and try not to sin again.

I want to follow you always but, like the little lost sheep, sometimes I go astray.

Please always come find me, lead me home, and keep me in your love.

Amen

This book belongs to

____

DO I ALWAYS FOLLOW JESUS?

Do I love God with all my heart, soul, and mind?

Have I remembered to pray to God every day?

Have I said God's name in a bad or unkind way?

Do I laugh if someone uses God's name in a bad or unkind way?

Have I done anything to hurt my own or someone else's body?

Have I taken anything that belongs to someone else?

Have I cheated in my school work or at home or during games?

Have I lied to anyone?

Do I remember that Sunday is God's day?

Do I say the Mass prayers as best I can?

Have I been disrespectful to my parents or other adults who take care of me?

Have I been angry or mean to anyone?

Have I failed to tell someone something that I know I should have?

Have I been jealous of what others have?

Have I been jealous of another person's family or lifestyle?

Name ______________________________

Meeting the Forgiving Jesus (Part 1)

Meet Jeffrey. He is going to Confession for the first time. He chose to go to Confession face-to-face. When Father speaks to him, what does Jeffrey say? Cut out and paste Jeffrey's word balloons where they belong.

Name ____

Meeting the Forgiving Jesus (Part 2)

Meet Maggie. She has just confessed her sins. Now Father will help her find ways she can make up for her sins. Then Maggie will say her Act of Contrition, and Father will give her a sign of God's forgiveness. Maggie will thank Jesus for his forgiving love. Cut out and paste Maggie's word balloons where they belong.

Thank you, Father, and thank you, Jesus.

Dear God, I am sorry for all my sins. Please forgive me. I promise to do better from now on. Amen.

I will be more helpful around the house. I will be more truthful.

Amen.

Name ____

I'm Sorry

Contrition means being sorry for something you did wrong. There are prayers you can say that tell God you are sorry for your sins. One of them is called the Act of Contrition. You say this prayer when you go to Confession. Here is an Act of Contrition you can say.

Dear God,

I am truly sorry for the unloving things I have done. When I remember how much you love me, I want only to love you in return. Please forgive me for my sins, and help me to sin no more.

Amen

Now write your own Act of Contrition. There are four things you should include in your prayer:

1. Tell God you are sorry.
2. Ask God to forgive you.
3. Remember God's love for you.
4. Ask God to help you to be good.

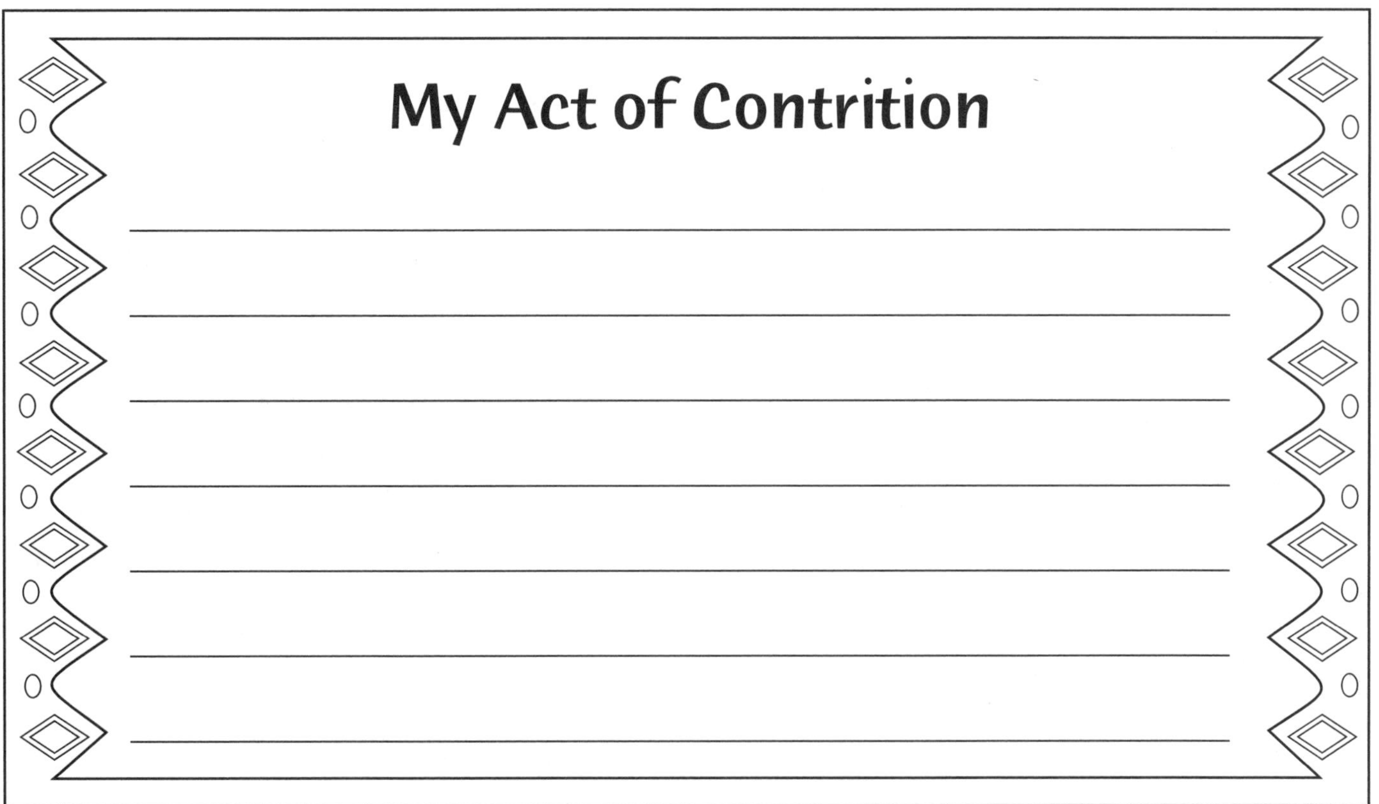

Name ____________________

I Follow Good Advice

When we go to Confession, after we tell the priest our sins and tell God we are sorry, Father talks to us about things we can do to atone for our sins. Atone means to make things right again. Father will tell us what to do and help us learn not to commit these sins again. This is called our penance.

Doing our penance shows that we are truly sorry and will try not to sin again. Below is a list of sins followed by a list of possible penances. Can you match the sin to the penance? Put the correct letter in the box following each sin.

Sin		Penance
I was giggling with my brother at Mass and didn't pay attention.	☐	A. Write an "I'm sorry" note to your mother.
I used the name of Jesus in anger.	☐	B. Tell your friend you are sorry you hurt his feelings.
I fought with my best friend.	☐	C. Say, "I'm sorry," to your sister and promise to ask her before you touch her things. Do something special for her.
I took my sister's new music box without asking.	☐	D. Learn this prayer and say it often: "Lord Jesus, I love your holy name."
I disobeyed my mother.	☐	E. Listen carefully to the readings at Mass. Later, tell your parents what the readings were about.
I told my friend his new jacket was dumb because I was jealous of it.	☐	F. Tell your friend you are sorry for fighting. The next time you are together, play your friend's favorite game.

Name ____

A Special Gift

Every time we confess our sins, tell God we are sorry, and do our penance, Jesus gives us a gift. This gift makes wonderful things happen for us and within us.

- It takes away the guilt we felt from our sin.
- It helps us to be strong when we are tempted to do wrong.
- It makes us feel closer to God.
- It inspires us to do good things for others.
- It fills us with peace.

To find the name of this wonderful gift from Jesus, solve this rebus using the line below to work on.

Working Line

That wonderful gift from God is called ___ ___ ___ ___ ___.

Name ______________________________

Hidden Messages

Sometimes it's hard to see what is hidden inside something else.

Sometimes wrong ideas look like good ideas.

Sometimes behaving badly looks like fun.

Sometimes we're told, "Go ahead, it's okay. Nobody will catch you."

When the right thing to do seems hidden, we can get all mixed up in our thinking. The word that describes these times is below, but the vowels are all mixed up. See if you can put them in the right place to spell the word that can mix up our thinking.

T O M P T E T A I N

T __ M P T __ T __ __ N

Now, using that word, see if you can find 4 two-letter words, 4 three-letter words, and 4 four-letter words hidden in it.

Two-letter Words

I T __ __ __ __ __ __ __ __

Three-letter Words

T A P __ __ __ __ __ __ __ __ __ __ __ __

Four-letter Words

T E A M __ __ __ __ __ __ __ __ __ __ __ __ __ __ __ __

Think of something you have been tempted to do that was wrong.
On the back of this page, write why it looked good to you or felt like the right thing to do.

Name ______________________________

Stop, Look, Listen, Act

What can we do…

- when something bad looks like fun?
- when something wrong looks right?
- when we know it's wrong but everyone else is doing it?

Here are four steps to take when we are tempted to do wrong.

1. Stop for a minute and think about it.

2. Look at whether it is right or wrong to do it.

3. Listen to what Jesus wants you to do. Ask him to help you.

4. Take action by walking away from the bad thing and doing something else.

You can use these four steps to solve this puzzle. You will learn the words Jesus gave us to say when we are tempted to do wrong.

S T O P — 6 9 8 17
F O R — 27 13 26
A — 3
M I N U T E — 16 10 7 5 12 2

L O O K — 1 22 22 —
A T — 19 14
R I G H T — 32 10 — 30 18

A N D — 3 11 4
W R O N G — — 32 22 23 —

L I S T E N — 1 21 6 20 15 7
T O — 29 24
J E S U S — — 31 6 25 6

T A K E — 14 3 — 2
A C T I O N — 28 — 9 10 13 7

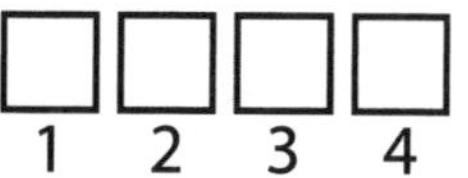

☐☐☐☐ ☐☐ ☐☐☐ ☐☐☐☐
1 2 3 4 5 6 7 8 9 10 11 12 13

☐☐☐☐☐☐☐☐☐☐.
14 15 16 17 18 19 20 21 22 23

Now find the name of the prayer Jesus gave us.

☐☐☐ ☐☐☐☐☐☐
24 25 26 27 28 29 30 31 32

Name ____________________

A Maze of Decisions

Learning to avoid temptations that cause us problems is very important.

See if you can get through this Maze of Decisions. Each time you come to a sign, think about the situation and choose the path that would help you avoid that temptation. See how wrong decisions lead you to the wrong path and right decisions help you win.

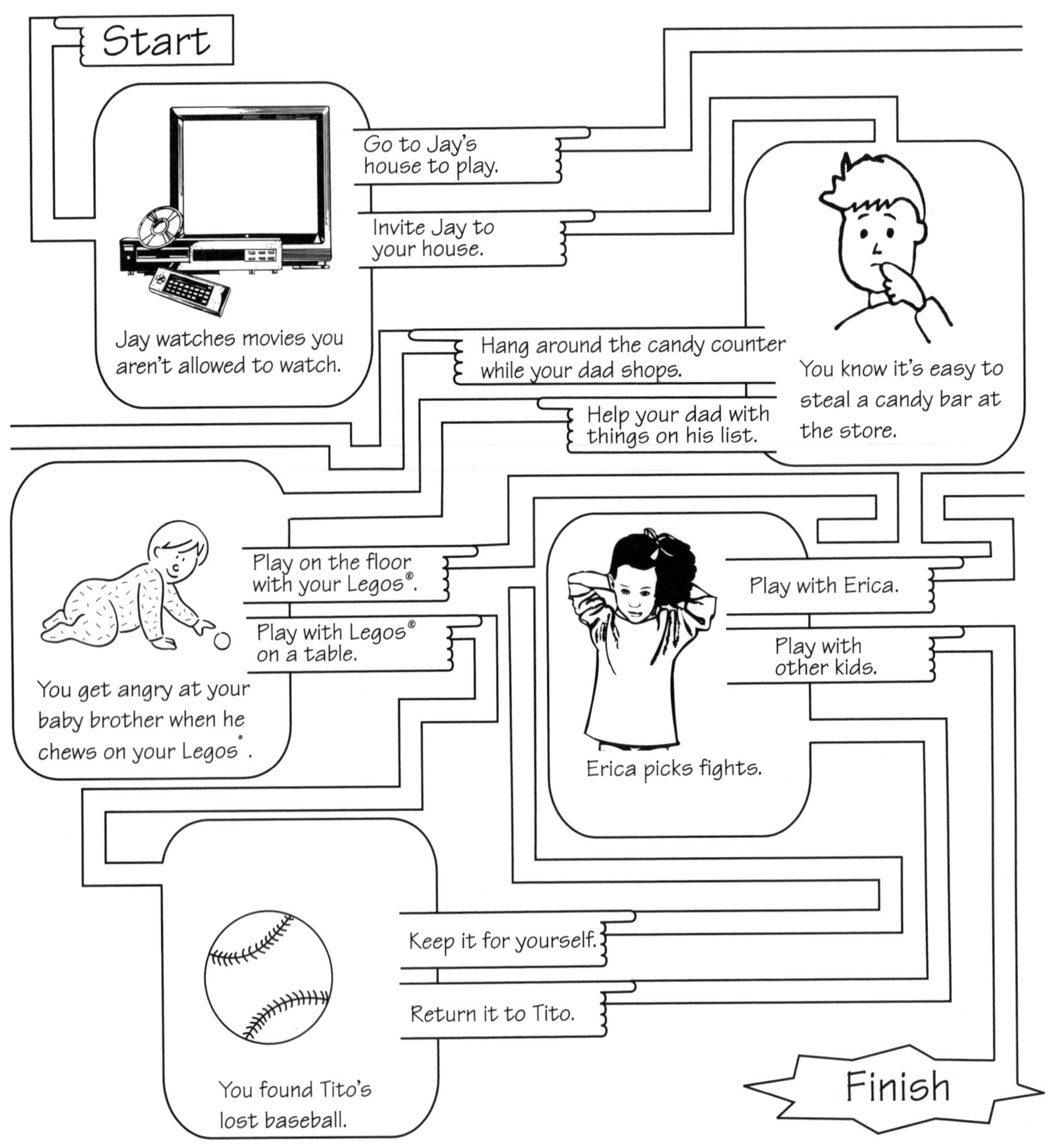

Name ____

Staying Strong

Jesus taught us how to stay close to God always.

Using the line below, solve this puzzle to see what it is Jesus tells us to do every day.

STOP + O + L - + S

+ + K + Y - =

Working Line

Answer:

___ ___ ___ ___

Make up a prayer telling God why you want to stay close always. Write it here.

Name ____

Staying Close to Jesus

It feels good to confess our sins and know that Jesus always forgives us. Being with our Church family helps us stay close to Jesus. Each time we go to Mass, we see things that remind us that Jesus is with us all the time.

Fill in the blanks with words from the Word List to find some things that remind us of Jesus when we go to Mass.

1. We bless ourselves with ________ ___________ and remember that we were baptized into God's family, just as Jesus was baptized.

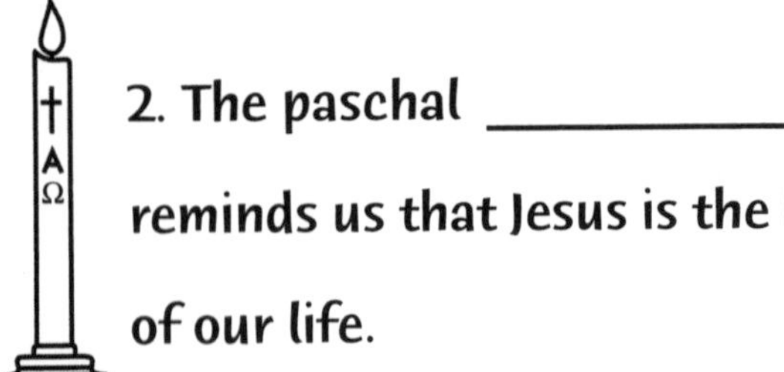

2. The paschal ______________ reminds us that Jesus is the light of our life.

3. The __________ makes us think of the table where Jesus and his disciples shared the Last Supper.

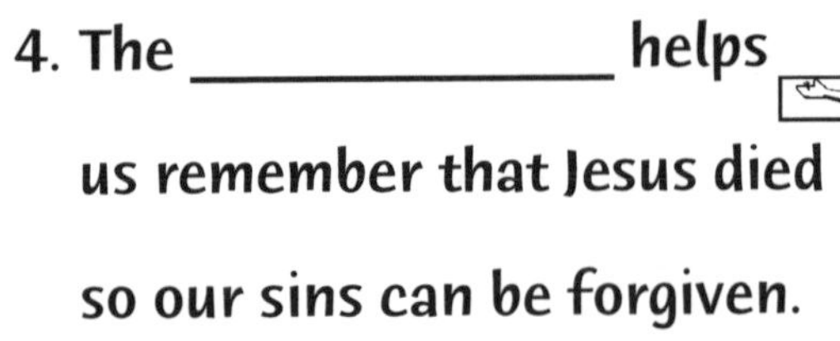

4. The ______________ helps us remember that Jesus died so our sins can be forgiven.

5. As we listen to the readings from the ________, we hear stories of God's love for us and of Jesus' life on earth.

6. The______________holds the Holy Eucharist, the gift Jesus gave us of himself.

7. The________, or plate, holds the bread that becomes the Body of Christ.

8. The__________, or cup, holds the wine that becomes the Blood of Christ.

Word List			
	Bible	altar	chalice
	holy water	crucifix	candle
	tabernacle	paten	

Answers and Notes

Page 5

What Makes You Happy?

This simple activity is a good way to review with the children that God made them to be happy.

Page 6

Following God

"Whoever does the will of my Father in heaven is my brother, and sister, and mother"(Matthew 12:50).

Page 7

Building Blocks of Love

This activity helps children connect the people in their lives with the ways they learn about God. Discuss each picture with the children. Scripture references are as follows: Love one another... (Luke 10:27). When two or three gather...(Matthew 18:20). Teach them... (Matthew 28:19-20). Forgive others (Luke 11:4). Pray always (Luke 18:1). Give to...(Luke 18:22).

Page 8

Rules Rebus (Part 1)

HOE + GG - EGG + BOWL - BOW + Y = HOLY

Page 9

Rules Rebus (Part 2)

TIRE + ES - TIE + CAPE - CA + CAT - A = RESPECT

Page 10

Jesus' Love in Motion

"Acting out" an important message is an excellent way for children to remember that message. Help the children learn the poem by leading them through the words and gestures until they are at ease with them.

Page 11

The Most Happy People

The Beatitudes can be found in Matthew 5:1-12 or Luke 6:20-26.

Supplies needed: paper plate; construction paper; glue; markers; paper punch; yarn or ribbon

Preparation:

Using the paper plate as a guide, trace a large circle onto a piece of construction paper for each child. You can also just use a paper plate for each child, but construction paper is more colorful.

Page 12

Accident, Mistake, or Sin?

It's important for children to recognize that not all "bad" things they do are sins.

Answers: 1. accident; 2. sin; 3. mistake; 4. sin; 5. accident

Page 13

The Key to Forgiveness

"Forgive and you will be forgiven." Discuss with the children times when they have been in need of forgiveness and when they have needed to forgive.

Page 14

Turning Bad into Good

This activity is based on Luke 6:27-28. Being nice to people who are not nice is a difficult concept for children, as well as for many adults. Use examples from your own experience, from children's stories, or from Scripture to help the children see how Jesus' words are true. Answers: 1. LOVE your ENEMIES. 2. DO GOOD to those who HATE you. 3. BLESS those who CURSE you. 4. PRAY for those who MISTREAT you.

Page 15

Forgive—Times Seven

E	V	I	G	R	O	F	O
E	F	F	I	V	E	G	E
V	E	O	F	O	G	V	I
I	F	O	R	G	I	V	E
G	E	V	I	G	R	O	F
R	G	I	R	O	I	F	I
O	E	O	O	I	E	V	V
F	F	O	R	G	I	V	E

Page 16

Signs of Peace

Ask, "What sign do we use at Mass to wish peace to those around us?" Discuss cultural customs that initiate or confirm peace.

Page 17

Listen to Your Heart

Children gradually learn that they are responsible for their own behavior. This activity helps them recognize the value of listening to their inner voice. Answer: It is called a conscience.

Page 18

Fresh Starts

Emphasize to the children how much better we feel when we are able to correct a problem and start over. Answers to the puzzles: Penance, Confession, Reconciliation

Pages 19-20

My Reconciliaton Book

Copy these pages back-to-back so that, when folded in half, the child will have a booklet. Pray the Prayer Before Confession together. Then go over each question in the examination of conscience. Add more questions as you see fit. Let the children complete their books by coloring the borders and filling in the blanks. Encourage the children to take the book with them to Confession and to say the Prayer after Confession.

Pages 21-22

Meeting the Forgiving Jesus

Try to arrange a visit to church to view the confessional. Explain the different ways of going to confession. Emphasize that it is the child's choice whether to go face-to-face or behind a screen.

Page 23

I'm Sorry

Having an Act of Contrition memorized can be very reassuring to some children, but it is also important for the children to know the reason for the prayer and how to say "I'm sorry" in their own words.

Page 24

I Follow Good Advice

It is important for children to remember that penance is not a punishment but an atonement. Ask the children for other examples of sins and appropriate penances. Answers in order: E, D, F, C, A, B

Page 25

A Special Gift

PIG + E - PIE + ROAD - O + FISH - DISH - F + ICE - I = GRACE

Page 26

Hidden Messages

Discuss what temptation is and why it is wrong to give into it. Invite the children to share the ideas they wrote down.

Page 27

Stop, Look, Listen, Act

Knowing short prayers to say at certain times is reassuring to children.
Answers: Lead us not into temptation. Prayer: Our Father

Page 28

A Maze of Decisions

For some decisions, there are no right or wrong answers. Offer other situations that need decisions and let the children discuss how they should react to them.

Page 29

Staying Strong

STOP + O + L – STOOL + S + RAIN + K + Y – SINK = PRAY

Page 30

Staying Close to Jesus

This activity helps the children learn the meaning behind some familiar things they see at Mass.
Answers: 1. holy water; 2. candle; 3. altar; 4. crucifix; 5. Bible; 6. tabernacle; 7. paten; 8. chalice